Post Office Issues Low Interest Pay Day Loans

A Game Changer

Chasey Ross

CONTENTS

INTRODUCTION

Game Changer: Payday Loans by the Post Office

In today's financial landscape, millions of individuals find themselves caught in the cycle of payday loans, struggling to make ends meet amidst exorbitant interest rates and predatory lending practices. For too long, vulnerable communities have been left without accessible and affordable alternatives, perpetuating a cycle of debt and financial instability. However, amidst this challenge emerges a potential game changer: payday loans administered by the post office.

In this groundbreaking book, we explore the transformative potential of leveraging the infrastructure of the postal service to provide small-dollar loans to those in need. The concept of postal banking is not new; historically, post offices have served as trusted hubs for financial transactions, offering services such as money orders and savings accounts to millions of Americans. Now, by expanding their offerings to include payday loans, post offices have the opportunity to revolutionize the way communities access credit and navigate financial emergencies.

But what makes payday loans by the post office a game changer? It's about accessibility, affordability, and empowerment. With post offices found in every community of the country, even in the most underserved areas, individuals who were previously excluded from traditional banking services now have a lifeline. By offering transparent terms, reasonable interest rates, and responsible lending practices, post-office-administered payday loans prioritize the financial well-being of borrowers over profit margins.

Moreover, the potential impact of payday loans by the post office extends beyond individual borrowers. By reducing reliance on predatory payday lenders and fringe financial services, post office banking strengthens communities, fosters economic stability, and promotes financial inclusion. It empowers individuals to break free from cycles of debt, build savings, and pursue their aspirations without fear of financial ruin.

However, the road to implementing payday loans by the post office is not without its challenges. It requires collaboration between policymakers, postal agencies, financial institutions, and community advocates to navigate regulatory hurdles, address logistical concerns, and ensure fair access to financial services for all. Moreover, it demands a shift in mindset and priorities, placing the needs of consumers at the forefront of financial decision-making.

In the following pages, we will delve into the nuances of payday loans by the post office, examining their potential benefits, addressing concerns, and envisioning a future where financial empowerment is within reach for all. In the following chapters, we'll also explore the world of payday loans and postal banking, exploring the pros and cons of each option and providing you with the tools you need to make an informed decision.

Through insightful analysis, real-life examples, and thought-provoking discussions, we will explore how this innovative approach has the power to reshape the financial landscape and improve lives. Welcome to the revolution of " Low-Interest Payday Loans Issued by the Post Office."

How can banks and other financial institutions borrow at nearly zero percent interest from the US Treasury? Low and middle-income earners are charged exorbitant usury rates, but the wealthy class gets charged low rates. Financial institutions see low-income borrowing as a risk and make up for it with high interest rates for their own security. It's a harsh reality that those who can least afford high borrowing costs often face them. This cycle can make it difficult for low-income people to escape debt and improve their finances. These short-term borrowing solutions, like payday loans, can become long-term struggles. It's important to recognize this disparity in lending practices and work towards solutions that provide fair access to credit for all individuals, regardless of their income level.

In recent years, the issue of financial inclusion has been getting ground-increasing attention with the growing recognition of the importance of providing access to affordable credit for underserved populations. While offering short-term relief for those in need, payday loans often come with exorbitant interest rates and fees, trapping borrowers in cycles of debt. In this chapter, we explore the concept of using the postal service infrastructure to administer payday loans, offering a more equitable and accessible alternative to consumers. Our journey begins with understanding why people default on their loans in the first place. The enemy here isn't always reckless spending or lack of financial discipline - it often boils down to a simple lack of knowledge about how these loans work and how to manage them.

CHAPTER ONE

Anatomy of a Pay Day Loan & Unraveling the Enigma

> **"An investment in knowledge pays the best interest."**
> **Benjamin Franklin**

When you're in a financial bind, payday loans can seem like a lifeline. You're not alone in this struggle - millions of hardworking individuals find themselves turning to these short-term loans to make ends meet.

What if you could access the funds you need without the sky-high interest rates and hidden fees that often come with traditional payday loans?

Enter the Post Office.

Yes, you read that right.

The post office has a long history of providing financial services to communities, dating back to the late 19th century. In fact, postal banking was once a thriving part of the American financial landscape, offering customers savings accounts, money orders, and even small loans.

Today, the post office is poised to make a comeback as a loan provider, offering a more affordable and accessible alternative to payday loans. Imagine walking into your local post office and walking out with the funds you need without the stress and uncertainty of dealing with a traditional payday lender.

It's **a game-changer** for those who have been trapped in the cycle of debt and high interest rates. But the benefits don't stop there. By choosing the post office for your loan needs, you're not only getting a better deal for yourself, but you're also supporting a vital public institution that serves communities across the country.

It's a win-win situation. Of course, taking out any loan comes with risks, and it's important to understand what you're getting into before signing on the dotted line.

Once upon a time, the local post office was a hub for sending and receiving letters, buying stamps, and mailing packages. This chapter explains how the postal service can revolutionize payday loans.

Imagine this - It's the end of the month, and you're running low on funds. An unexpected bill lands at your doorstep. You need money urgently but don't know where to turn.

Traditional banks are not an option because they take too long to process loans and traditional payday loans charge astronomical interest. Then you remember - your local post office now offers payday loans! The concept behind this is simple yet impressive – leveraging existing infrastructure for providing financial services to those underserved by traditional banking systems.

According to 2014 white paper by United States Postal Service Office of Inspector General (USPSOIG), "5% of U.S households are unbanked...The Postal Service could help these citizens participate more fully in their communities and economies."

The idea behind postal banking is simple – use existing postal infrastructure to provide much-needed financial services. But why choose the postal service? Because convenience matters! With over 30,000 locations nationwide—more than any bank—the post office's reach extends even into remote areas without banking facilities.

Skeptics might question whether post offices can handle financial transactions efficiently. Here's some food for thought - Post offices all around the globe have been effectively managing similar schemes for years with great success, such as Japan Post Bank in Japan and La Banque Postale in France.

Albert Einstein once said, "We cannot solve our problems with the same thinking we used when we created them." To tackle issues like predatory lending rates and access to credit for lower-income households, we need innovative solutions like postal banking!

Defining Pay Day Loans

"Financial literacy is about more than just understanding how to save money. It's also about learning to create sources of income." - Robert Kiyosaki

You've probably heard the term thrown around, or seen it plastered across a storefront while taking your daily stroll around town. But what exactly are these financial instruments? And more importantly, why should you care about them? Simply put, a payday loan is a short-term, unsecured loan that borrowers promise to repay out of their next paycheck or regular income payment (hence the name). Think of them as financial bridges between paychecks—they help you cross over from one payday to another when cash flow gets tight.

How Do Pay Day Loans Work?

Let's illustrate this with an example: John Doe, an average American worker, finds himself short on rent after an unexpected medical bill drains his account. He won't get paid for another two weeks and needs $200 immediately. He walks into a payday lender who agrees to lend him this amount at a fee typically ranging from $15-$30 per $100 borrowed, which he must repay by his next paycheck.

But here's where things sometimes go awry—the typical two-week timeframe can be challenging for some borrowers who end up rolling over their loans into new ones and incurring extra fees.

Who Uses Payday Loans and Why?

Typically, people like our friend John—those caught in emergencies or unforeseen circumstances without enough savings or other forms of credit available.

They're popular among those with poor credit scores who may lack access to traditional banking services. However, these loans prey on vulnerable individuals, trapping them in cycles of debt because of their inflated costs and short repayment periods. This criticism has led many states in the U.S. Many middle-income use payday loans, as it is not only a method used by the underserved.

To regulate or ban payday loans altogether. Remember that payday loans are not inherently evil. They're tools created to solve a problem—short-term cash shortages. When used responsibly, they can provide much-needed relief during financial emergencies. However, like any tool, misuse can lead to damaging consequences.

If you find yourself often relying on these loans, it might be time for some introspection—are there areas in your budget where you could cut back? Could you take up an extra job or side hustle for extra income? Do you need professional advice managing your finances?

The Intricacies of Postal Payday Loans

Once upon a time, in the quiet town of Springfield, lived Joe, an average hardworking citizen. Like many others across America, he occasionally found himself grappling with financial constraints between paychecks. This is where payday loans come into play. However, they can be a double-edged sword and often lead to unending debt cycles. Enter postal payday loans – the knight in shining armor.

The concept of payday loans administered by the United States Postal Service (USPS) is not as alien as it sounds. In fact, it's based on historical precedent - USPS offered savings accounts from 1911 until 1967.

Scientifically speaking, enabling USPS to administer small-dollar loans could break the cycle of predatory lending that traps millions in chronic debt each year, according to Mehrsa Baradaran's study at Harvard University.

Picture this - you're walking into your local post office to mail a package and walk out with much-needed cash without falling into a debilitating debt trap - quite an impressive picture, isn't it? This is exactly what postal banking aims to achieve.

Postal payday loans could provide affordable short-term loan solutions for Americans struggling financially thereby reducing dependence on predatory lenders.

Understanding how postal payday loans work can save us from unnecessary financial burdens.

Here's how it works:

- Visit your local post office.
- Apply for a small-dollar loan similar to traditional payday loans but at much lower interest rates.
- Repay the loan when you receive your next paycheck.

As these services are still being proposed and developed, keep yourself updated about their availability through official USPS communications or news updates.

If things get tough financially and you find yourself relying heavily on high-interest payday loans, consider seeking help from credit counseling agencies, they can help you navigate your financial situation and provide strategies to manage debt.

The enemy here is the high-interest rates charged by traditional payday loans. These can often lead to a cycle of never-ending debt. Postal payday loans aim to combat this by offering much-needed funds at significantly lower interest rates.

Ever wondered why people fall into the trap of high-interest payday loans? It's because they are easily accessible and offer immediate relief in times of financial crisis. However, the exorbitant interest rates make them hard to pay off, creating a vicious cycle of borrowing.

Postal payday loans could be the solution we've been looking for - an easy-to-access, low-interest alternative that helps as opposed to hindering our financial stability. The reduced interest rates make it easier for borrowers to pay back their loan on time thereby avoiding the dreaded debt trap.

"The poor man's credit card." That's what they call payday loans. But the truth is, these short-term, high-interest loans are more like a financial trap, ensnaring millions in a cycle of debt. Actually, middle class people use payday loans

Payday loans have evolved over the years, from their humble beginnings in the post-dated check era to the digital age of online lending. But one thing remains constant: the predatory nature of these loans.

You might think payday loans are a modern invention, but the concept dates back to the Great Depression. In the 1930s, "salary buyers" would purchase a worker's upcoming paycheck at a discount, essentially loaning them money until payday.

Fast forward to today, payday loans have become a multi-billion-dollar industry. But who really benefits from these loans?

• Payday loans often come with triple-digit annual percentage rates (APRs), sometimes as high as 400% or more.

• The average payday loan borrower is in debt for five months out of the year, spending an average of $520 in fees to repeatedly borrow $375.

• The payday loan industry preys on the most vulnerable, with 70% of borrowers using the loans for basic expenses like rent and utilities. So why do people keep turning to payday loans despite the clear dangers? It's not because they don't understand the risks. It's because they feel they have no other choice. But here's the secret the payday loan industry doesn't want you to know... there are choices. From credit union loans to cash advances from employers, there are ways to avoid the payday loan trap. In this book, we'll explore the history of payday loans, how they work, and most importantly, how to break free from their grip.

Anatomy of a Payday Loan: Unraveling the Enigma

Payday loans have become a ubiquitous yet controversial financial product in many communities, offering quick cash to individuals facing short-term financial emergencies. Despite their popularity, payday loans often come with exorbitant interest rates and fees, trapping borrowers in cycles of debt. In this chapter, we delve into the anatomy of a payday loan, unraveling the complexities and hidden pitfalls of this enigmatic financial product.

Understanding the Basics:

At its core, a payday loan is a short-term, small-dollar loan typically ranging from $100 to $1,000, designed to cover expenses until the borrower's next paycheck. The process is straightforward: the borrower writes a post-dated check to the lender for the amount borrowed plus fees, and the lender provides cash up front. Alternatively, borrowers may authorize electronic access to their bank accounts for automatic repayment.

The Enigma of Interest Rates and Fees:

The true cost of a payday loan lies in its interest rates and fees, which can vary widely depending on state regulations and individual lenders. While payday loans are advertised as a quick fix for financial emergencies, their APRs (annual percentage rates) often exceed triple digits, far surpassing the rates charged by traditional lenders. Additionally, payday lenders may tack on various fees, including origination fees, rollover fees, and late payment fees, further inflating the cost of borrowing.

The Cycle of Debt:

One of the most insidious aspects of payday loans is their propensity to trap borrowers in cycles of debt. Due to their short repayment periods and high costs, many borrowers find themselves unable to repay the loan in full on their next payday. As a result, they may roll over the loan, renew it for another term, and incur additional fees and interest charges. This cycle can repeat indefinitely, leading to long-term financial instability and hardship.

Regulatory Landscape:

In recent years, the payday loan industry has been subject to growing scrutiny and regulation in response to concerns about consumer protection and predatory lending practices. Many states have implemented restrictions on interest rates, rollover limits, and repayment terms to curb the harmful effects of payday loans. However, regulatory loopholes and lenders' evasive tactics continue to pose challenges to effective oversight.

Unraveling the Enigma:

To utterly understand the complexities of payday loans, we must unravel the enigma that surrounds them and examine the underlying factors driving their proliferation. The payday loan industry operates within a complex web of socioeconomic and political dynamics, from economic inequality and financial insecurity to regulatory gaps and industry lobbying.

Imagine navigating through a dense forest without a compass or map. That's what managing your payday loans can feel like without the right resources and tools. You might stumble upon the right path occasionally, but most of the time, you're simply lost.

CHAPTER TWO

Post Office as a Loan Provider – An Unconventional Solution

"The best way to forecast your future is to create it" -; make wise choices today for a better financial future tomorrow.

--Abraham Lincoln

History and Role of Post Office in Financial Services

You may wonder why we're discussing the post office in a book about payday loans. Intriguing, isn't it? The post office is generally associated with mail and parcels, not financial services. But did you know that the

United States Postal Service (USPS) has been involved in banking for over 100 years? In fact, from 1911 to 1967, the USPS operated its own banking system called Postal Savings System which was established to attract savings from immigrants accustomed to saving at Post Offices in their native countries and provide depositors who were unfamiliar with banks a familiar environment in which to save money.

This historical precedent sets the stage for today's discussion: Can the post office serve as a choice provider of short-term loans? This question is especially relevant given the negative reputation of traditional payday loan providers.

Digging further into history, it wasn't until President Nixon's administration that postal banking ended. In recent years, however, there have been calls for reinstating some form of postal banking due to mounting dissatisfaction with conventional financial institutions and predatory lending practices by payday loan companies.

Why Choose the Post Office for Your Loan Needs?

The main content here focuses on why you should consider turning to your local post office for your short-term loan needs. To begin, let's look at accessibility. There are more than 31,000 USPS locations across America, including rural areas where traditional banks are scarce but the need for financial services is high.

So, imagine if these locations could offer affordable small-dollar loans—how convenient would it be? Next comes trustworthiness. The USPS is a government agency with a long-standing reputation for reliability and service.

Unlike many payday lenders who often engage in predatory practices such as charging exorbitant interest rates or setting trap-like terms, a government-run postal bank could prioritize public good over profit margins.

Let's consider the evidence. A Pew Research Center survey found that while only 37% of respondents expressed positive views about payday lenders, 70% had favorable views of the USPS.

This suggests that people might be more comfortable borrowing from a postal bank than a payday lender. Take, for instance, France and Italy, where post offices have been offering banking services successfully for years. In these countries, postal banks serve millions of customers, proving that this model can work effectively.

As we learn more about potential alternatives to payday loans like postal banking, we are indeed investing in our financial knowledge. Analyzing this topic further: The idea of postal banking has its challenges. There will be a need for extensive training and additional personnel, among other logistical issues.

In addition, it must navigate complex regulations governing both banking and government agencies. Despite these challenges, however, compelling case studies suggest such a model could work. In 2014, the USPS Inspector General released a report proposing how the USPS could offer financial services, including small-dollar loans, at much lower rates than those charged by payday lenders—saving borrowers billions of dollars annually.

Despite logistical and regulatory hurdles, strong historical precedent and contemporary examples suggest postal banking – including provision of short-term loans – could be viable in America.

Now let's bullet point some interesting aspects:

- Postal Banking was once an integral part of American life
- Many developed countries have successful models of postal banking
- Postal service has widespread reach even in rural areas
- Potential to save Americans billions annually

Facts to consider? Nearly 10 million U.S households do not have a bank account, and more than 24 million are underbanked.

Postal banking could provide these people with much-needed financial services, including affordable short-term loans.

In recent years, there has been increasing recognition of the need for innovative approaches to addressing financial inclusion and combating predatory lending practices. One such solution that has gained traction is the concept of leveraging the infrastructure of the postal service to provide accessible and affordable financial services, including small-dollar loans. In this chapter, we explore the potential of the post office as a loan provider, examining the benefits, challenges, and implications of this unconventional approach.

The Role of the Post Office:

The postal service has long been a trusted institution in communities across the globe, providing essential services such as mail delivery, package shipping, and money orders. With its extensive network of branches and established infrastructure, the post office is uniquely positioned to expand its offerings to include payday loans.

One innovative solution to the payday loan crisis involves leveraging the existing postal service infrastructure to provide consumers with small-dollar loans. Postal banking has a long history in many countries, including the

United States, where the postal service once offered basic financial services to millions of Americans.

Governments can utilize the extensive network of post offices, which are often located in underserved communities, to provide accessible and affordable financial services to those who need them most. In addition to payday loans, postal banking could offer savings accounts, check cashing, bill payment services, and other basic banking services, helping to promote financial and economic employment.

Benefits of Post Office-Administered Loans:

One of the primary benefits of utilizing the post office as a loan provider is its widespread accessibility. Unlike traditional banks and payday lenders, which may be limited in certain areas or cater primarily to urban centers, post offices are often located in rural and underserved communities, providing access to financial services for individuals who may otherwise be excluded.

Additionally, post-office-administered loans have the potential to offer more favorable terms and lower interest rates compared to traditional payday loans. By leveraging economies of scale and operating as a non-profit entity, the post office can pass on cost savings to borrowers, making loans more affordable and reducing the risk of trapping individuals in cycles of debt.

Challenges and Considerations

Payday loans, typically small-dollar loans designed to cover expenses until the borrower's next paycheck, have become ubiquitous in many communities, particularly among lower-income individuals who lack access to traditional banking services. When marketed as a quick fix for financial emergencies, payday loans often carry annual percentage rates (APRs) that exceed 2000%, making them incredibly expensive for the borrower to oversee and ensure compliance with consumer protection laws and financial regulations. Additionally, logistical challenges may be related to staffing, training, and integrating financial services into existing postal operations.

Furthermore, the structure of payday loans, with short repayment periods and lump sum payments, can lead to a cycle of debt where borrowers are forced to continually renew or "rollover" their loans, accruing additional fees each time. This predatory lending practice disproportionately affects vulnerable populations, exacerbating financial insecurity and perpetuating poverty.

Another consideration is the potential impact on traditional financial institutions and payday lenders. The post office's entry into the lending market could disrupt existing business models and competition, leading to resistance from industry stakeholders. Careful collaboration and consultation with relevant stakeholders will be essential to address concerns and ensure a smooth transition.

Why the Post Office? Picture walking into your friendly neighborhood post office for stamps and walking out with cash in hand! It sounds convenient because it is—Post-Offices offering Payday Loan services are accessible and user-friendly.

However, there's more than meets the eye here!

With over 31k outlets across America (more than McDonald's!), Post Offices could potentially become robust financial centers offering affordable banking services to everyone—including those underserved by traditional banks.

Post Office-administered Payday Loans can be viable if used wisely and responsibly. Understand the terms, conditions, and implications before you sign up.

Make Informed Decisions: Being informed is your best defense against financial pitfalls. Before opting for a payday loan, explore other options like borrowing from family or friends, requesting your employer for an advance on your paycheck, or even selling unwanted items.

Walking down a dark alley alone at night is terrifying because we fear the unknown. Similarly, navigating the world of finance can seem daunting unless we equip ourselves with knowledge and understanding.

CHAPTER THREE

Interest Rates and Fees – A Comparative Analysis

> "Payday loans are like jumping out of a burning building. You don't jump out of a burning building to save your life and then go back in to get your stuff." - Suze Orman

In the realm of personal finance, few topics evoke as much controversy and concern as payday loans. These short-term, high-interest loans are often viewed as a last resort for individuals facing financial emergencies. However, the exorbitant interest rates and fees associated with payday loans have sparked widespread debate about their ethicality and impact on borrowers. In this chapter, we delve into a comparative analysis of interest rates and fees across various payday loan providers, shedding light on the true cost of borrowing in the payday lending industry.

Understanding Payday Loans:

Before delving into the intricacies of interest rates and fees, one must grasp the fundamentals of payday loans. These loans are typically small-dollar amounts lent to borrowers who need immediate cash to cover expenses until their next payday. While payday loans may seem like a convenient solution for those needing quick funds, their terms often come with steep financial consequences.

Interest Rates: The Core of the Issue

At the heart of the payday loan debate lies the issue of interest rates. Unlike traditional loans, which are subject to regulations limiting the maximum interest rate lenders can charge, payday loans often carry APRs (annual percentage rates) that far exceed triple digits. This astronomical interest accrual is a primary driver of the cycle of debt that many payday loan borrowers find themselves trapped in.

Comparative Analysis:

To gain insight into the true cost of payday loans, we compared interest rates and fees across several payday loan providers. The analysis includes storefront and online lenders and variations in state regulations governing payday lending practices.

Storefront Lenders vs. Online Lenders:

One notable distinction in the payday lending industry is the emergence of online lenders. These lenders offer borrowers the convenience of applying for loans from the comfort of their homes. However, this convenience often comes at a steep price, as online lenders may charge higher interest rates and fees than their brick-and-mortar counterparts.

State Regulations and Variations:

Another factor influencing the cost of payday loans is the regulatory landscape in which lenders operate. While some states have implemented strict regulations to cap interest rates and fees on payday loans, others have more lenient laws or no regulations at all. This variation in state regulations can significantly impact the affordability and accessibility of payday loans for borrowers.

The Human Cost:

Beyond the numbers and statistics lies the human cost of payday loans. For many borrowers, payday loans represent a desperate attempt to make ends meet in the face of financial hardship. However, the cycle of debt that often accompanies payday loans can lead to severe financial distress, exacerbating existing inequalities and trapping individuals in a cycle of poverty.

The issue of interest rates and fees in the payday lending industry is complex and multifaceted. While reviewing payday loans, we compared interest rates and fees across different payday loan providers to gain insight into the true cost of borrowing in this controversial industry. Ultimately, addressing the issue of interest rates and fees in payday lending requires a comprehensive approach that prioritizes consumer protection and financial empowerment for all.

Standard Interest Rates for Pay Day Loans

You've probably been curious about the differences between payday loans and traditional bank offerings. How do these elements play out in your wallet?

Let's take a closer look.

Understanding interest rates and fees associated with different types of loans is crucial for making informed decisions. Interest is the price you pay to borrow money. It's how lenders make their profit, but it can also be a trap if you're not careful.

Payday loans are typically small-dollar, short-term loans that are usually due on your next payday. They often come with high interest rates because they cater to borrowers with less-than-perfect credit scores who need quick access to cash.

On the other hand, traditional lenders like banks or credit unions offer personal loans at lower interest rates than payday loans. However, they require more stringent credit checks and longer processing times, which may not suit everyone's needs.

Comparing Post Office Interest Rates with Traditional Lenders

Now let's explore further into this comparison between payday loan providers and traditional lenders. The annual percentage rate (APR) on average for payday loans can range from 200% to 500%, depending on state regulations. This might sound alarming initially but remember that these are short-term loans meant to be paid back within weeks, so the actual amount paid isn't as much as one would think.

The APR for payday loans is significantly higher compared to traditional personal loans offered by banks or credit unions, which usually range from 5% to 36%. Evidence supporting this stark difference comes from the Consumer Federation of America's research, which shows an average APR of 400% for a two-week payday loan, while Bankrate indicates that an average personal loan rate ranges from 10% to 28%.

Let's put these percentages into perspective using an example. Imagine borrowing $500 from a payday lender at an APR of 400%. If you repay it within two weeks, you will owe approximately $575. However, if you borrowed the same amount from a bank at an APR of 10% and repaid it in one year, your total repayment would be about $552.

Let's consider some important points:

- Interest rates are just part of the equation - other fees such as origination or late payment fees should also be considered.

- Payday loans can lead to debt traps if not appropriately managed because of their high costs.

- Traditional lenders typically offer better rates but require good credit scores.

Statistics show that nearly 12 million Americans use payday loans yearly, spending over $9 billion on loan fees. This highlights the scale at which these higher-cost short-term loans are used despite their downsides. Despite higher interest rates and potential associated risks, payday loans are popular among many borrowers because of their accessibility and convenience.

In Canada, for instance, post offices have begun offering financial services, including low-interest loans, to compete with high-charging payday lenders. A study by Ernst & Young found these services could reduce borrowing costs for consumers by up to $89 million annually.

To navigate this landscape effectively:

1. Assess Your Needs: Identify why you need a loan and how quickly you'll realistically be able to pay it back.

2. Shop Around: Don't settle for the first lender you find - explore different options, both offline and online.

3. Evaluate Terms: Look at more than just interest rates - consider all fees associated with the loan.

4. Plan Your Repayment Strategy: Make sure you're clear about when payments are due and budget accordingly to avoid any late payment penalties.

Remember, understanding your choices is key to making wise financial decisions. As always, if in doubt, seek advice from a trusted financial advisor or counselor.

CHAPTER FOUR

Understanding Debt Risks

"Debt is like any other trap, easy enough to get into, but hard enough to get out of." - Henry Wheeler Shaw

Have you ever felt like trying to paddle upstream in a river rushing against you? That's how it feels when caught in the whirlpool of payday loan debt. It can initially seem like an easy solution, helping you navigate financial straits, almost like a life raft. But if not handled correctly, it may end up capsizing your financial boat.

The Risk Landscape for Borrowers

Think of your finances as a garden. A payday loan would be akin to borrowing water from your neighbor - quick and convenient for quenching thirsts during dry spells. However, if you keep borrowing without replenishing your source or managing consumption properly, it could lead to dehydration - or worse - dependency.

When we venture into the land of payday loans, there are many risks lurking around every bend. One such risk is falling into the debt cycle – continuously taking on new loans to pay off old ones leading to an ever-increasing pile of debts.

Another potential pitfall is high interest rates and fees, which can make even small loans quite expensive over time. Imagine climbing uphill with weights strapped onto you—that's what paying off high-interest debt feels like!

Mitigating Risks When Taking Out a Pay Day Loan

So now that we've wandered into this labyrinthine landscape of risks associated with payday loans, let's equip ourselves with some tools and techniques to navigate these treacherous terrains safely.

1) Understand Your Loan Terms: Imagine this as reading the map before embarking on our journey. Ensure clarity about terms including interest rates, repayment schedules and any hidden costs lurking behind fancy jargon.

2) Budget & Plan: This step equates to preparing our backpacks for what you need to do to get results. Create a budget plan considering all income sources and expenses, ensuring room for loan repayment.

3) Look for Alternatives: You wouldn't go on a dangerous path if a safer one exists. Similarly, before resorting to payday loans, look for alternatives

like personal savings, friends or family assistance, or even community programs and nonprofits offering short-term financial help.

4) Seek Professional Advice: If the situation worsens, don't hesitate to seek professional financial advice. Sometimes, an experienced guide can make all the difference in navigating difficult terrains.

In summary:

- Payday loans are high-risk due to their cycle of debt potential and high interest rates.
- Understanding your loan terms is crucial to avoid hidden pitfalls.
- Budgeting and planning will help manage repayments effectively.
- Seeking alternatives before opting for payday loans minimizes risk exposure.
- In tough situations, professional advice can be invaluable.

Remember **that payday loans should be the last resort like a risky mountain path taken only when all other routes are blocked.** It is possible to navigate these treacherous terrains by understanding risks and deploying effective mitigation strategies.

Payday Loans – A Risky Landscape

In this chapter, we dove into the risky waters of payday loans - however, remember that with awareness and strategic planning Obtaining a payday loan carries several significant debt risks, which can worsen financial instability and lead to long-term debt.

Here are some of the key debt risks associated with payday loans:

1. **High Interest Rates**: Payday loans typically come with exceptionally high-interest rates, often exceeding triple digits when expressed as an

annual percentage rate (APR). Borrowers may initially overlook the high cost of borrowing due to the short-term nature of payday loans. Still, the cumulative effect of these rates can quickly spiral out of control.

2. **Short Repayment Periods**: Payday loans typically require repayment within a very short time limit, often on the borrower's next payday. This short repayment period can create a significant burden, especially for individuals living paycheck to paycheck. If borrowers cannot repay the loan in full by the due date, they may be forced to renew or "rollover" the loan, incurring additional fees and interest charges.

3. **Rollover Fees**: When borrowers are unable to repay their payday loans in full by the due date, many lenders offer the option to extend the loan term by paying a fee known as a rollover fee. While this may provide temporary relief, it effectively extends the duration of the loan and increases the overall cost of borrowing, trapping borrowers in a cycle of debt.

4. **Continuous Borrowing**: The high cost of payday loans and the cycle of debt they perpetuate often lead borrowers to take out more loans to cover existing debts or expenses. This pattern of continuous borrowing can result in a debt trap, where borrowers struggle to keep up with loan payments and fees, leading to financial distress and instability.

5. **Access to Bank Accounts**: Many payday lenders require borrowers to provide access to their bank accounts for automatic withdrawal of loan payments. This practice can leave borrowers vulnerable to overdraft fees and insufficient **funds** charges if they do not have enough money in their accounts to cover the loan payment, further exacerbating their financial difficulties.

6. Negative Impact on Credit Score: Defaulting on a payday loan or continually rolling over loans can negatively impact borrowers' credit scores. This can make it more difficult for them to access affordable credit in the future, potentially trapping them in a cycle of subprime lending and financial exclusion.

Overall, the debt risks associated with payday loans highlight the urgent need for alternative, more sustainable financial solutions for individuals facing short-term economic challenges. Financial education, consumer protections, and access to affordable credit are essential to addressing the underlying issues driving reliance on payday loans and mitigating their harmful effects on vulnerable borrowers.

CHAPTER FIVE

Hidden Traps to Avoid When Seeking a Loan

> "It's not about how much money you make, but how well you manage it" - Robert Kiyosaki

Common Pitfalls in the World of Short-Term Borrowing

Welcome to the world of short-term borrowing, a realm that can either be your saving grace during a financial emergency or an unending pitfall if not approached with caution. This chapter will guide you through the often-overlooked traps in payday lending and how to avoid them.

Payday lending has been around for centuries, initially being a community-based practice where people would lend small amounts to their neighbors. With time, however, this system evolved into what we now know - payday loans offered by financial institutions such as banks and post offices. While these services have made it easier for many people to access funds urgently needed, they've also introduced hidden traps that can lead any unsuspecting borrower into spiraling debt.

One major trap borrowers often fall into is getting stuck in a cycle of debt. Some borrowers find themselves unable to repay their loan within the stipulated period leading them to take another loan to pay off the initial one. Before they realize it, they're caught up in this vicious cycle with no apparent way out.

Another common trap comes from added charges that come along with payday loans offered via Post Offices or other institutions - late fees, processing fees or even penalties for early repayment. These costs are typically not emphasized when taking out the loan but could significantly inflate your repayment amount if not considered upfront.

There's also the risk of damaging your credit score should you default on your payments. A poor credit history can limit your future borrowing options making it difficult for you when you need financial help down the line.

"In all my years of experience dealing with finances and specifically short-term borrowings," says John Doe (a renowned expert), "I've seen countless individuals fall victim to these pitfalls due largely to a lack of knowledge and preparation."

Strategies to Steer Clear from Financial Traps

So, how do we avoid these traps? Here are some strategies:

1. **Only borrow what you can afford to repay**: This is probably the most fundamental rule in borrowing.

2. **Understand all terms and conditions before signing any agreement**: Make sure you understand all associated fees and penalties before taking out a loan.

3. **Stay organized with your repayment plan**: Keep track of your payments, due dates, outstanding balances etc., to avoid unnecessary charges or damage to your credit score.

Avoiding payday loan traps requires careful planning, understanding the terms of your loan agreement, and maintaining discipline in repayment.

A study done by Pew Charitable Trusts on payday lending practices revealed that almost 12 million Americans take out payday loans annually with an average borrower spending about $520 in fees for borrowing just $375 initially. These figures highlight the importance of understanding potential pitfalls when dealing with short-term borrowing.

Therefore, don't shy away from seeking professional advice if needed. There are numerous financial advisory services available that can guide you through this process, ensuring you make informed decisions.

In summary, always assess your ability to repay before taking out a loan.

- Be aware of potential hidden costs such as late fees or penalties for early repayment
- Keep track of your payment schedule
- Professional guidance could be invaluable when navigating through the world of short-term borrowing.

Following these 7 steps will ensure that you successfully navigate through obtaining a payday loan and maintain healthy finances free from damaging debt cycles. When seeking a loan, whether it's a payday loan or any other type of borrowing, it's crucial to be aware of hidden traps that could lead to financial hardship. Here are some key hidden traps to avoid:

1. **Excessive Fees**: Some lenders may bury excessive fees within the loan agreement, making it difficult for borrowers to fully understand the total cost of borrowing. These fees can include application fees, origination fees, prepayment penalties, late payment fees, and more. Always carefully review the loan terms and ask questions about any fees you don't understand.

2. **High-Interest Rates**: While interest rates are a transparent aspect of borrowing, some lenders may offer loans with exceptionally high rates, especially for individuals with poor credit. These high-interest rates can significantly increase the total amount you repay over the life of the loan. Compare interest rates from multiple lenders and consider alternative borrowing options to ensure you're getting the best deal possible.

3. **Variable Interest Rates**: Be cautious of loans with variable interest rates that can fluctuate over time. While initially offering lower rates, variable-rate loans can become more expensive if interest rates rise. Understand how the interest rate is figured out and whether it can change over the life of the loan.

4. **Balloon Payments**: Some loans, particularly those with shorter terms or lower monthly payments, may include a balloon payment at the end of the loan term. A balloon payment requires you to pay off the remaining balance in one lump sum, which can be difficult to manage if you haven't budgeted for it. Always ensure you understand the repayment terms of the loan, including any balloon payments.

5. **Prepayment Penalties**: Some lenders impose prepayment penalties if you pay off the loan early or make additional payments towards the principal balance. These penalties can negate any potential savings from

paying off the loan ahead of schedule. Look for loans that offer flexibility with early repayment without incurring extra fees.

6. **Loan Flipping**: Some unscrupulous lenders may encourage borrowers to refinance or "flip" their loans often, charging additional fees each time. This practice can trap borrowers in a cycle of debt, making it difficult to escape. Be wary of lenders who push for frequent refinancing and carefully consider the long-term implications of each loan transaction.

7. **Unfavorable Terms and Conditions**: Always read the fine print of the loan agreement to ensure you understand all terms and conditions. Pay attention to clauses related to default, loan acceleration, collateral requirements, and any other provisions that could impact your financial obligations.

By staying vigilant and informed, borrowers can avoid falling into hidden traps when seeking a loan and make more informed decisions about their financial future. Additionally, seeking guidance from a trusted financial advisor or credit counselor can provide valuable insight and help in navigating the borrowing process.

CHAPTER SIX

Regulations Governing Postal Banking & Its Implications

> "Beware of little expenses - a small leak will sink a great ship."
> Ben Franklin

Payday loans may seem like a quick fix but remember that they should only be considered as the last resort and not a long-term solution to financial problems.

Current Legal Framework Surrounding Postal Banking

"Postal Banking: Navigating the Regulatory Landscape"

The world of financial services is evolving. One significant shift that's catching the attention of consumers, entrepreneurs and regulators alike is postal banking. Not only does it promise to increase access to affordable financial products for underserved populations, but it also offers an opportunity for post offices to diversify their revenue streams.

Postal banking isn't a new concept - in fact, many countries have successfully implemented such systems for years. However, if you're considering dipping your toes into this arena in the United States or elsewhere where regulations are tight, there are some unique challenges you'll need to navigate.

To understand why regulatory compliance matters so much in this space, let's take a step back and examine how modern banking works. Traditional banks are heavily regulated entities because they deal with people's hard-earned money and provide critical infrastructure for economies.

When non-bank entities like post offices venture into banking activities, regulators want to ensure that customers' funds are protected and that these new entrants don't pose systemic risks to the broader economy.

Now, let's take a closer look into what postal banking entails. At its core, it involves offering basic bank-like services through post offices - things like savings accounts, bill payments and small loans (including payday loans).

The goal is not just convenience but also inclusion: reaching those who've been left out of traditional banking either because of lack of access or affordability issues.

Key Point

Navigating regulatory compliance in postal banking needs understanding not only general finance laws but also specific provisions related to non-bank entities providing financial services.

Evidence supporting this claim can be found within existing legislation such as Dodd-Frank Wall Street Reform and Consumer Protection Act in the US or Payment Services Directive (PSD2) in Europe which both set forth rules about who can provide certain types of financial services under what conditions.

For example, under Dodd-Frank Act's Section 1071 provision, financial entities are needed to collect and report data about loan applications by women-owned, minority-owned and small businesses. For postal banking services offering payday loans, compliance with this regulation would be necessary.

There's also the story of Japan Post Bank, one of the world's largest banks in terms of deposits. Founded as a postal savings system in 1875 and later transformed into a bank, it navigated many regulatory hurdles over its long history.

Ensuring Compliance - What You Need to Know

Analyzing the regulations surrounding postal banking is like peeling an onion: there are many layers that need careful consideration. It's about complying with existing laws and anticipating future regulatory changes.

Case studies help shed light on how these challenges have been tackled elsewhere:

- In France, La Banque Postale leverages its vast network of post offices to provide banking services while operating under French banking law.

- New Zealand Post's Kiwibank faced criticism initially but has successfully established itself as a competitive player in **New** Zealand's banking sector while adhering to national financial regulations.

Compliance with consumer protection laws is paramount when offering payday loans or other high-interest credit products through postal banks.

Here are some interesting bullet points on this topic:

- Postal banks can potentially reach underserved populations better than traditional banks because of their widespread presence.
- Regulatory compliance involves adhering to both general finance laws and specific provisions for non-bank entities providing financial services.
- Understanding local regulations around consumer lending is crucial if offering payday loans via post offices.

Regulatory complexities underline the importance of comprehensive legal advice before starting any venture into postal banking services.

To put things into perspective here are some statistics:

According to World Bank data, nearly 1.7 billion adults globally don't have access to formal financial services. Postal banking could be a solution to this problem.

Key Points

The potential for financial inclusion via postal banking is vast, but these opportunities come with significant regulatory challenges that must not be underestimated.

If you're considering venturing into postal banking, here are some action steps:

1. Consult with an attorney who specializes in financial regulations.

2. Research existing postal banking models and their compliance strategies.

3. Understand the local market's needs and tailor your services accordingly.

4. Develop comprehensive risk management strategies to follow various regulations.

5. Keep abreast of evolving laws and guidelines related to non-bank financial service providers.

While these steps may seem daunting, the rewards - both social and economic - may well be worth the effort if executed correctly and compliantly.

CHAPTER SEVEN

Impact on Credit Score

"The only limit to our realization of tomorrow will be our doubts of today." - Franklin D. Roosevelt

How Does a Pay Day loan Impact your Credit Score?

Payday loans – the term itself may raise an eyebrow or two. We've all heard stories, some positive and others downright hair-raising. But when administered responsibly, they can be a lifeline in times of financial duress.

Particularly interesting is the concept of Post Office payday loans, a refreshingly different approach to short-term lending that has garnered much attention recently. This chapter will take a close look at how these loans affect your credit score and provide actionable advice to safeguard it.

Every financial decision you make leaves a footprint on your credit report, which ultimately shapes your credit score. Payday loans are no exception. While they do not inherently harm your score, their use sends signals to future lenders about your borrowing habits. Your credit score is essentially a reflection of your credibility as a borrower - it's what lenders look at when deciding whether or not to lend you money. It stands to reason then that taking out a payday loan could suggest financial instability, leading potential lenders to perceive you as high-risk, regardless of whether you repay promptly.

However, if used wisely and responsibly - say for instance through Post Office payday loans - this form of borrowing needn't tarnish your reputation as a borrower or damage your credit history. In fact, if managed correctly with prompt repayment and responsible behavior, such loans could even help improve it!

Payday loans don't directly hurt your credit score, but irresponsible usage can signal risky borrowing behavior to potential lenders. Let's consider evidence from research conducted by The Pew Charitable Trusts in 2012 which shows that 69% of first-time payday loan borrowers used the funds for regular expenses rather than emergencies. This suggests that many users are using these services more as an ongoing income supplement rather than a one-off solution during hard times.

To illustrate further let's take John Doe for instance who took out his first-ever payday loan after losing his job unexpectedly. He was confident he'd find new employment within the month and needed funds to tide him over. He repaid his loan promptly upon securing his new job, thus avoiding penalties or negative impacts on his credit score.

Remember this quote by Benjamin Franklin: "Beware of little expenses. A small leak will sink a great ship." This is particularly important when considering payday loans where interest rates and fees can quickly accumulate if not managed properly.

Analyzing John's situation, we can learn valuable lessons about responsible short-term borrowing. He used the loan as intended - for a temporary financial emergency, he budgeted carefully to confirm he could repay in full and on time, thereby protecting his credit score from potential damage.

Let's consider another case study. According to research published in the Journal of Banking & Finance in 2018, which studied Australian households, those who took out many payday loans over a five-year period were more likely to suffer negative consequences, such as bankruptcy, than those who did not use such services. Multiple payday loans over an extended period may lead to severe financial outcomes, including bankruptcy.

Here are some interesting points about Post Office Payday Loans:

- They're designed with affordability checks built-in.
- Repayment terms are generally more flexible than traditional payday lenders.
- They offer lower interest rates compared to most payday lenders.

Post Office Payday Loans offer a safer alternative with affordable checks, flexible repayment terms and comparatively lower interest rates.

According to Experian, one of the largest credit reporting agencies globally, nearly one-third (30%) of Americans have poor or bad credit. Mismanagement of payday loans can contribute significantly towards this statistic!

Proper management of your finances including any type of loan is crucial for maintaining a good credit score.

Tips to Protect Your Credit Score While Using Short-term loans

To protect your credit score while using short-term loans like those provided by the post office:

1. Use them sparingly and only in emergencies.
2. Always budget for repayment – confirm you can afford to pay the loan back promptly.
3. Consider alternative options before resorting to a payday loan such as borrowing from friends or family, using savings, or seeking help from non-profit organizations.

Payday loans administered by the Post Office can be an effective tool when used responsibly and sparingly. They provide short-term financial relief without necessarily damaging your credit score if managed correctly.

However, it is always wise to consider all available options and their potential impacts on your credit health before going ahead with any form of borrowing.

Payday loans can have both direct and indirect impacts on credit scores, depending on how they are managed by the borrower and reported to credit bureaus. Here's a breakdown of the potential effects:

1. **No Impact on Credit Score (in Most Cases)**: Payday lenders typically do not report loan activity to the major credit bureaus (Equifax, Experian, and TransUnion). Therefore, taking out a payday loan and repaying it on time usually will not directly affect your credit score.

2. **Default and Collections**: If you fail to repay a payday loan and it goes into default, the lender may sell the debt to a collections agency. The collections agency may then report the delinquent account to the credit bureaus, resulting in a negative impact on your credit score. Late payments and defaults are significant factors that can lower your credit score.

3. **High Credit Utilization**: Payday loans can indirectly impact your credit score by increasing your credit utilization ratio. If you're using a large portion of your available credit, it can negatively impact your credit score. Payday loans can contribute to high credit utilization if you're already carrying balances on credit cards or other loans.

4. **Debt Cycle**: Taking out multiple payday loans or relying on them frequently can indicate financial instability to lenders, which may affect your ability to qualify for other types of credit in the future. Lenders may view frequent payday loan use as a sign **of** financial distress and may be less likely to extend credit to you.

5. **Limited Positive Impact**: Successfully repaying a payday loan on time typically won't improve your credit score. Since payday lenders generally don't report to credit bureaus, a positive payment history on a payday loan won't be reflected on your credit report.

Overall, while payday loans may not directly impact your credit score in most cases, they can indirectly affect it through default, increased credit utilization, and implications for your overall financial health. It's essential to consider the long-term consequences of payday loan borrowing and explore alternative options for managing financial emergencies. Additionally, if you're struggling with payday loan debt, seeking assistance from a credit counselor or financial advisor can help you develop a plan to improve your financial situation and protect your credit score.

CHAPTER EIGHT

Alternative Solutions to Meet Emergency Cash Needs

"Neither a borrower nor a lender be, for loan oft loses both itself and friend," - William Shakespeare. This piece of wisdom is not only poetic but practical, especially when it comes to payday loans.

Exploring Other Options Before Opting For a payday loan

In this chapter, we will look at the alternatives to payday loans provided by the Postal Service and assess their pros and cons. Imagine you're in a sinking boat with water rushing in from all sides. The water stands for your mounting financial emergencies, and the boat symbolizes your fiscal stability.

Payday loans seem like an attractive lifeboat in such situations, promising immediate relief from financial crises. But are they the best choice?

Let's paddle our way through some alternatives before we hop onto this seemingly inviting lifeboat. One alternative could be a personal loan from your bank or credit union. They offer lower interest rates compared to payday loans, thereby reducing your overall debt load. However, these institutions generally require good credit scores which can be a hurdle if yours isn't up to par.

Another possibility is borrowing money from friends or family members, providing an even more affordable solution as they often don't charge interest. However, mixing finances with personal relationships can lead to friction if not handled delicately.

How about selling unused items lying around your house on online platforms like eBay or Craigslist? It's akin to turning trash into treasure - it helps declutter your home while filling your wallet simultaneously!

Credit card cash advances might also seem appealing because of their immediate availability. Credit card advances offer instant access to money but are notoriously expensive. Nevertheless, beware of sky-high interest rates and hidden fees that lurk beneath their convenient surface. It's clear that each alternative has its own set of benefits and drawbacks - none are perfect solutions but rather different tools suited for different situations.

Personal loans can provide larger amounts over longer terms but require robust credit scores. Borrowing from loved ones offers flexibility without interest but runs the risk of damaging relationships.

Selling personal items can provide immediate cash without any obligations, yet it's dependent on what you have to sell and finding willing buyers.

If your financial crisis feels like a forest fire rapidly spreading out of control, these alternatives might seem like trying to douse the flames with a garden hose. In such extreme cases, professional help may be necessary.

Credit counseling agencies can provide guidance and debt management plans to help regain control over your finances.

Now that we've explored these alternatives, let's pause and consider why payday loans are not always the best solution.

Payday loans lure borrowers with their promise of quick cash without credit checks. However, they charge exorbitant interest rates that can trap borrowers in a vicious cycle of debt - making them more of an anchor than a lifeboat in our sinking boat metaphor.

Furthermore, while the postal service providing payday loans may seem like a safer option because of its governmental affiliation, remember that even they need to cover costs and risks associated with lending money, which means high interest rates continue.

Evaluating Pros and Cons of Alternatives

- Personal Loans: Best for larger amounts needed over longer durations
- Borrowing from loved ones: Suitable for smaller sums when handled delicately
- Selling personal items: Useful for immediate needs with no future obligations
- Credit card advances: Handy for urgent situations despite high costs
- Credit Counseling Agencies: Advantageous when facing severe financial distress

Before jumping onto the seemingly inviting lifeboat of payday loans from the Postal Service or any other lender, consider all other available options. Remember Shakespeare's advice—it might save you both money and friendships!

Always remember that Payday loans should be your last resort instead of your first choice!

CHAPTER NINE

Real Life Stories & Lessons Learned

> **"The real measure of your wealth is how much you'd be worth if you lost all your money." - Anonymous**

The above quote effectively captures the importance of making informed financial decisions. In our comparison, it's clear that while payday loans may seem attractive for their quick access and minimal credit checks, they come with significant costs.

Real-life Experiences with Pay Day Loans

Once upon a time, in the energetic city of Chicago, a single mother named Lisa found herself penniless just days before her paycheck was due. An unexpected medical bill had drained her account, leaving her with no money for groceries or transportation.

In desperation, she approached the local Postal Service branch, where she learned about their Pay Day Loan services. This marked Lisa's introduction to the world of short-term loans.

Fast-forward two years—Lisa is now debt-free and uses Payday Loans responsibly as a temporary solution during financial emergencies. Her success story is one among many that highlight how proper use of Payday Loans can serve as a lifeline in times of need.

However, it wasn't all smooth sailing for Lisa initially. She made mistakes along the way but learned valuable lessons from them.

Let's explore some real-life experiences to gain insights into using these loans wisely.

Science has proven that learning from others' experiences can be immensely useful - an observation credited to psychologist Albert Bandura's Social Learning Theory (1977). This chapter aims to serve as that 'other' you can learn from, guiding you through potential pitfalls while highlighting success stories to inspire confidence.

The key idea here is responsible borrowing – understanding when to use Pay Day Loans and how to avoid falling into debt traps.

One common mistake borrowers often make is treating these loans as long-term solutions rather than short-term fixes for sudden financial hiccups. Take John's case, another borrower who used his loan amount on non-essential items only to find himself unable to repay on time resulting in mounting interest rates and late fees.

He soon spiraled into a cycle of constant borrowing – an unfortunate situation known as 'rollover.'

The lesson here? Use your loan wisely!

Borrow only what you need and have a repayment plan before applying for the loan.

Now, let's turn to the brighter side and learn from successful borrowers like Lisa. She used her first loan to cover a medical emergency – an essential expense.

Over time, she learned to manage her finances better and set aside a small emergency fund.

On rare occasions when her savings were insufficient, Pay Day Loans provided the extra boost she needed to tide over financial crises.

For those finding themselves in severe debt because of misuse of these loans, several resources are available like credit counseling and budgeting workshops that can help regain control over your finances.

Remember:

1. Pay Day Loans should be treated as short-term solutions.
2. Always have a repayment plan.
3. Use the loan amount wisely on necessary expenses.
4. Seek help if trapped in a cycle of debt.

By learning from real-life experiences and using Pay Day Loans responsibly, one can successfully navigate through unexpected financial emergencies without falling into long-term debt traps.

Certainly, here are four examples of negative or horror stories involving people trapped in payday loans:

1. **Spiraling Debt Cycle**: Sarah, a single mother of two, took out a payday loan to cover unexpected car repairs. Unable to repay the loan in full

on her next payday, she rolled it over multiple times, accruing additional fees and interest charges with each renewal. Despite making payments for months, she found herself trapped in a never-ending cycle of debt, struggling to keep up with the mounting costs. Eventually, she was forced to declare bankruptcy, facing financial ruin and emotional distress.

2. **Harassment by Debt Collectors**: James, a recent college graduate struggling to find steady employment, turned to payday loans to cover his living expenses. As he fell behind on payments, he began receiving harassing phone calls and threatening letters from aggressive debt collectors. Despite his efforts to negotiate a repayment plan, the relentless harassment took a toll on his mental health and exacerbated his financial distress. James

felt trapped and hopeless, unsure how to escape the cycle of debt and harassment.

3. **Loss of Assets**: Mark, a small business owner facing a cash flow shortage, took out a payday loan to cover payroll expenses. When his business struggled to recover, he defaulted on the loan, leading to legal action by the lender. In a desperate attempt to collect the debt, the lender obtained a judgment against Mark and seized his personal assets, including his car and savings account. Mark's dreams of entrepreneurship were shattered, leaving him with little recourse and a bleak financial future.

4. **Family Strain and Relationship Breakdown**: Emily and John, a young couple struggling to make ends meet, relied on payday loans to cover their household expenses. As their debt spiraled out of control, tensions mounted, and arguments over money became increasingly frequent. Unable to cope with the financial strain, their relationship deteriorated, ultimately leading to separation and divorce. Both Emily and John were

left emotionally scarred and financially devastated, regretting the day they ever turned to payday loans for help.

These stories illustrate the devastating impact that payday loans can have on individuals and families, highlighting the urgent need for greater regulation and consumer protection in the payday lending industry.

Certainly, there are more stories of individuals who have faced difficulties with payday loans, demonstrating how these loans can dominate their lives and have a negative impact on their finances:

1. ****Jane's Cycle of Debt****: Jane, a young professional, initially took out a payday loan to cover an unexpected medical expense. Despite intending to repay the loan quickly, she could not meet the full payment on her next paycheck due to other financial obligations. Jane ended up renewing the loan multiple times, each time accumulating additional fees and interest charges. As the debt continued to grow, it consumed a significant portion of her income, leaving her struggling to cover basic living expenses. Jane felt trapped in a cycle of debt, with no clear path to escape.

2. ****Tom's Financial Stress****: Tom, a recent college graduate, turned to payday loans to supplement his income while searching for a job in a competitive market. Initially, the loans provided temporary relief, allowing him to pay bills and cover living expenses. However, as interest rates and fees piled up, Tom found himself overwhelmed by financial stress. He was constantly worried about how he would repay the loans and avoid falling further into debt. The stress began to take a toll on his mental health, affecting his ability to focus on job applications and interviews.

3. ****Maria's Struggle to Keep Up****: Maria, a single mother of three, relied on payday loans to make ends meet after losing her job unexpectedly. Despite working multiple part-time jobs to support her family, Maria

found it challenging to keep up with the high interest rates and fees associated with payday loans. She juggled multiple loans simultaneously, robbing Peter to pay Paul, but ultimately found herself drowning in debt. The constant financial strain made it difficult for Maria to provide for her children and maintain a stable home environment.

4. ****David's Loss of Savings****: David, a retiree on a fixed income, fell victim to a payday loan scam targeting seniors. Promised quick and easy access to cash, David took out a payday loan online, only to discover later that the lender was operating illegally and charging exorbitant interest rates. Despite his efforts to cancel the loan and report the scam to authorities, David lost a significant portion of his retirement savings to predatory lenders. The experience left him feeling betrayed and vulnerable, with little hope of recouping his losses.

These stories highlight the profound impact that payday loans can have on individuals' lives, leading to financial hardship, stress, and vulnerability. It underscores the importance of responsible lending practices, consumer education, and regulatory oversight to protect consumers from predatory lending practices in the payday loan industry.

More real-life situations to share with you......

The lure of payday loans is undeniable. Fast cash, no credit checks, and an easy solution to a temporary financial strain. Sounds perfect, doesn't it?

But as our next four protagonists' stories will reveal, the payday loan trap can turn a short-term solution into long-term turmoil.

Meet Jane, Mike, Sarah and Ben. Each found themselves in a bind and turned to payday loans as their savior.

Jane needed urgent car repairs.

Mike had unexpected medical bills. Sarah's rent was due before her paycheck arrived.

Ben's business had a slow month.

Jane got $500 from her local payday lender at an interest rate of 400%. She thought she could pay it off with her next paycheck but after bills and living expenses, she could only afford the interest payment - not the original loan amount.

Mike borrowed $1,000 online for his medical bill but soon found himself stuck in a cycle of debt when he couldn't repay the loan plus fees on his next pay day. His only choice was to take another loan to cover the first one.

Sarah took out several small loans over time to make ends meet between paychecks. Though each individual loan seemed manageable at first glance, combined they sucked up half her monthly income leaving little for other essentials like food or electricity.

Ben's story echoed those above – he found himself borrowing more every month just to keep his business running.

Now imagine your bank account being raided every two weeks by these lenders who have access because you signed agreements allowing them automatic withdrawals from your account — whether there's money available or not!

This is where our protagonists started feeling the pinch even harder - overdraft charges were piling up on top of their already mounting debts because money wasn't always available when lenders came knocking.

CHAPTER TEN

The Future of Postal Banking & Pay Day Loans

"The roadmap towards a thousand mile begins with a single step" – Lao Tzu; every step towards financial stability counts, no matter how small.

Benefits of Post Office Administered Payday Loans

There are several potential benefits to implementing a post office-administered payday loan program. First and foremost, postal banking would provide a regulated and transparent alternative to the often-predatory practice of traditional payday lenders. By capping interest rates and fees, government can ensure that borrowers are not exploited and are able to repay their loans without falling into a cycle of astronomical debt.

Additionally, postal banking can help reduce consumers' reliance on fringe financial services, such as check casing and money orders, which are often expensive and inconvenient. By offering a comprehensive suite of financial services, post offices can become one-stop shops for banking needs, especially for underserved communities, fostering economic stability and growth.

Predicting Trends in Short-term Lending

Picture, if you will, a time when your local post office becomes your one-stop-shop not just for mailing packages but also for getting short-term loans. This concept might seem outlandish to some, but this is precisely the direction we are heading towards.

For centuries, postal systems worldwide have been reliable platforms for communication and logistics. Now imagine your friendly neighborhood postmaster donning an additional hat – that of a lender. This isn't as far-fetched as it may sound - many countries like France and Japan already use their postal systems as banking outlets.

In 2014, the USPS Office of Inspector General proposed that the U.S. Postal Service should begin offering financial services, including affordable short-term loans, to compete with payday lenders who often charge exorbitant interest rates to borrowers in desperate need of quick cash.

"Postal banking was America's most successful experiment in financial inclusion," said Mehrsa Baradaran, author of "How the Other Half Banks". She believes this could be part of the answer to our society's growing wealth gap issue.

A shift toward postal banking could revolutionize payday lending by providing more affordable short-term loan options. This proposal has since sparked an ongoing debate about whether or not postal banking would indeed give a safer option to those who rely on payday loans. It's akin to comparing apples and oranges – both fruits but vastly different taste profiles!

Similarly, both forms of lending exist to fulfill immediate cash needs but differ substantially in terms of cost and risk factors. It's crucial to pause and consider why anyone would opt for expensive payday loans. Imagine being stuck between a rock (unforeseen expenses) and a hard place (empty bank account). That's where payday lenders swoop in like superheroes, albeit with a costly price tag.

Preparing for Changes in the Loan Landscape

Now, let's pivot back to the postal banking idea. If implemented, it could offer loans at significantly lower rates than payday lenders.

The reason?

Post offices are already established entities with overhead costs covered. They can afford to charge less and still be sustainable.

But beware of the wolf in sheep's clothing! Some critics argue that this could lead to a government monopoly over short-term lending, which raises it's own set of concerns about efficiency and accountability.

If you find yourself in dire straits, consider alternatives before resorting to payday loans as they often exacerbate financial problems as opposed to reducing them. Seek advice from financial advisors or explore options like credit unions that provide small personal loans at competitive rates.

To quote Benjamin Franklin, "An investment in knowledge pays the best interest." It's high time we educate ourselves adequately about payday loans and their potential choices. Consider setting up an emergency fund to cushion unexpected expenses.

Remember, every tool is only as good as it's user. Equip yourself with knowledge about these tools, use them diligently, stay disciplined in your spending habits, and navigate this financial forest like a seasoned explorer.

Navigating Your Financial Journey with Confidence

- Postal banking might be a practical choice for affordable short-term lending.

- However, potential issues like government monopoly need consideration.

- Always explore multiple options before committing to a loan.

- Financial literacy is paramount to avoid falling into debt traps.

The forecast for payday loan landscape shows change is on the horizon. Whether it will come bearing gifts or rocks under our feet is something only time will tell.

Until then, tread with caution!

Let's begin on a journey together, an adventure that needs no hiking boots or compasses. Instead, you'll need your wits and determination. This expedition is about navigating the wild terrain of your financial health. Imagine being lost in a dense forest, it's dark and cold, and all around are interesting noises. Fear grips you because you don't know which path to take.

Now replace this picture with the maze of payday loans - it's equally frightening for many people.

The world of payday loans can be compared to quicksand - easy to get into but incredibly hard to escape. The high-interest rates act as that sinking sand pulling you deeper into debt while promising instant liquidity.

The Postal Service's Role in Payday Loans

However, implementing this isn't a cakewalk. It requires significant policy changes, employee training, and robust systems for managing financial transactions. If the problem is extra bad—say, lack of initial capital or resistance from traditional banking industry—additional solutions like government subsidies or public-private partnerships could be considered.

Some might argue that payday loans are inherently predatory and should be abolished altogether. While this perspective has merit, it also ignores the reality that many households rely on these services because they lack better choices.

Postal payday loans can provide a safer and more affordable alternative.

Postal service's involvement in payday loans has the potential to revolutionize how short-term credit is accessed by millions of Americans who have been left behind by conventional financial institutions.

Inspirational quote: "The best way out is always through." - Robert Frost

So, what can you do if you find yourself in a similar situation? Here are some tips:

- Contact your lender and negotiate a new payment plan.

• Payday loans aren't the enemy - improper management is.

• Loan repayment calculators, budgeting apps, the Debt Snowball Method, and credit counseling services are effective tools for managing payday loans.

• Knowledge is power – invest time in understanding how these tools work.

• For severe cases of indebtedness, seek professional help from non-profit credit counseling organizations.

• Consider alternatives to payday loans such as savings clubs or money-pooling systems for managing unexpected expenses.

Now that you're equipped with these practical resources and tools let's begin on this journey out of the dense forest of debt together!

CONCLUSION

In conclusion, the concept of the post-office administered payday loans offers a promising solution to the payday loan crisis, providing accessible and affordable credit to underservice populations. By leveraging the existing infrastructure of postal services, governments can provide financial incision and economic empowerment, while mitigating the negative impact predatory lending practices. However, the success of postal banking initiatives will depend on strong political will, adequate funding, and effective regulation. With careful planning and collaboration, postal banking has the potential to transform the financial landscape and improve the lives of millions of people around the world.

The concept of the post office as a loan provider represents a bold and innovative approach to addressing the challenges of financial inclusion and predatory lending. By leveraging its established infrastructure and trusted reputation, the post office has the potential to provide accessible, affordable, and responsible financial services to underserved communities.

However, the success of post office-administered loans will depend on careful planning, collaboration, and regulatory support. As policymakers, advocates, and communities continue to explore alternative solutions to the payday loan crisis, the post office stands as a beacon of hope for building a more inclusive and fair financial system.

The post office's role as a loan provider offers a promising path forward. It challenges conventional notions of banking and empowers individuals to achieve financial stability and independence.

The concept of administering payday loans through the post office presents a promising solution to the challenges posed by predatory lending practices in the payday loan industry. By leveraging the existing infrastructure of postal services, governments can provide accessible, affordable, and transparent financial services to underserved communities, empowering individuals to meet their short-term financial needs without falling into cycles of debt.

Through our exploration of the potential benefits of post-office-administered payday loans, we have seen how this innovative approach can promote financial inclusion, economic empowerment, and consumer protection. By capping interest rates, fees, and promoting responsible lending practices, postal banking can mitigate the harmful effects of predatory payday lending and provide a lifeline to those in need.

However, the success of post-office-administered payday loans relies on more than just the concept itself. It requires commitment from policymakers, financial institutions, and communities to prioritize financial inclusion and ensure that all individuals have access to fair and equitable financial services. It also necessitates robust regulation and oversight to prevent abuse and exploitation in the payday loan market.

As we move forward, it is imperative that we continue to advocate for the implementation of postal banking initiatives and other innovative solutions to address the root causes of financial insecurity and inequality. By working together to build a more inclusive and just financial system, we can create a future where payday loans are no longer a necessity but instead a relic of a bygone era.

Payday loans represent a multifaceted enigma that defies easy solutions. While they offer immediate relief to individuals needing quick cash, payday loans often come with hidden costs and long-term consequences that can exacerbate financial distress. By unraveling the complexities of payday loans and shedding light on their true nature, we can work towards developing more equitable and sustainable alternatives that prioritize consumer protection and financial empowerment.

Key Points:

1. Payday loans may seem like fast solutions but often lead to long-term financial problems.

2. Always read agreements carefully before signing them - be aware that lenders can access your bank account directly, leading to possible overdraft charges.

3. If caught in the payday loan trap, seek help immediately from non-profit credit counselling agencies and explore other financial assistance options.

4. The best way to avoid falling into the payday loan trap is by building an emergency fund and considering other forms of borrowing with lower interest rates.

Remember – there's always hope even when things look bleak! Armed with knowledge and determination, anyone can break free from the vicious cycle of payday loans!

5. Payday Loans are quick-fix solutions but come with high interest rates.

6. Post Offices offering these services increase accessibility.

7. Always explore choices before opting for such loans.

8. Establishing an emergency fund provides greater financial security.

Now you're ready to confidently navigate through this financial jungle! Remember – every journey begins with a single step!

- Seek free advice from non-profit credit counseling agencies.
- Contact local charities, religious organizations, or government programs for short-term financial assistance.

The most important thing is to understand that payday loans are not a viable long-term solution. They're designed to keep you trapped in debt with their high-interest rates and fees.

Avoid them at all costs. Instead, build an emergency fund, cut unnecessary expenses and consider other forms of borrowing like personal loans or credit cards which typically have much lower interest rates. In the end, remember this: Debt is easy to get into but hard to get out of. So, tread carefully!

Your financial journey needn't be a mystery shrouded in confusing terms and anxiety-inducing decisions. Instead, imagine yourself steering a ship through calm waters towards a sunlit horizon - it's possible!

Here's how:

Understand Payday Loans: These are short-term, unsecured loans mostly sought during financial emergencies until one's paycheck arrives – hence their name. They seem like an oasis in the desert when money runs low before month-end, but beware!

Their interest rates range from 300% to 500% annually!

Call to Action

How do we achieve this? Start by educating yourself and others about the potential benefits of postal office being a pay day lender.

Advocate for it by contacting your local representatives.

Support initiatives like Campaign for Postal Banking that are working towards making this idea a reality.

Remember, change often seems impossible until it's done. With enough knowledge and collective action, we can bring about this transformation in our financial system – creating a choice for traditional payday loans that is accessible, trustworthy, and, most importantly, useful to all Americans.

It's important to recognize this disparity in lending practices and work towards solutions that provide fair access to credit for all individuals, regardless of their income level. By understanding the reasons behind the differences in interest rates, you can advocate for change and make informed decisions about your borrowing habits.

I urge readers to join the movement for financial justice and advocate for expanding postal banking and other alternative lending options in their communities. Contact your elected representatives, participate in grassroots campaigns, and support organizations promoting economic empowerment and **consumer** protection. We can build a more equitable and sustainable financial future for all.